The Eye
of the Prophet

The Eye
of the Prophet

KAHLIL GIBRAN

Translated from the French by
Margaret Crosland

Frog, Ltd.
Berkeley, California

The Eye of the Prophet

This book is a translated selection of writings from *L'Oeil du Prophete* by Kahlil Gibran, published in France by Editions Albin Michel. French translation by M. Dahdah, copyright © 1991 by Editions Albin Michel.

Contents

The Eye
of the Prophet

Quest for the Return

I have lived from the alpha of Creation and I shall live until the omega of Eternity. And my existence shall never wither away.

I have floated in the universe of the infinite and flown in the upper air of the imaginary world. There I was close to the circle with its divine light; here, I am in the prison of matter.

I have listened to the teachings of Confucius and the wisdom of Brahma. And I have been with Buddha in the shade of the Knowledge-Tree. And now I face ignorance and apostasy.

I have climbed Mount Sinai where in the past Jehovah rose up before the eyes of Moses. I have purified my body in the Jordan and I have lived through the miracles of the Nazarene. And at Medina I have listened to that Messenger repeat the Word in Arabic. And now I am undecided.

I have known the strength of Babel, the glory of Egypt, and the splendor of the Greeks. And perpetually I see weakness and servility, always present in all these creations.

I have kept company with the magicians of Ayn Dour.

Elsewhere I have been the guest of the Assyrian hermits, and I have followed the prophets in the land of Palestine. And still I am searching for the truth.

I have learned wisdom revealed in India and poetry breathed forth in Arabia. And I have heard the melodies that formed in the hearts of the countries where the sun is dying. And I see myself as still blind and I remain deaf to the sound of my unspeaking lips.

I have endured the ferocity and greed of conquerors and I have suffered beneath the yoke of tyrants. And I remain a force which fights at the stroke of every minute.

I have seen and heard all that when still a child, and I shall continue to look and listen to all the shallow deeds of my youth. Once my hair is white I shall brush against the fringes of fulfillment and I shall regain the dwelling of Allah.

If you are dead, he will restore life to you.

And if you die again, he will raise you up until the hour comes for your return to him.

A Winged Word

There is within me a friend who consoles me every time that troubles overwhelm me and misfortunes afflict me. The man who does not feel friendship towards himself is a public enemy, and he who finds no confidant within himself will die of despair. For life streams out of man's inner self and in no way from what surrounds him.

I have come in order to say one single word, and I shall say that word today. But if death were to prevent me from doing so, then it will be said Tomorrow. For Tomorrow will leave no secret in the book of Eternity.

I have come in order to live in the glory of Love and in the light of Beauty. On this earth I live, and no one can drive me away from the spheres of Life. If my eyes are torn, I shall feel joy as I listen to the songs of Love and the melodies of Beauty. And if my ears are cut off I shall feel pleasure in touching the upper air, in the sighs of lovers and the fragrance of Beauty. And finally if my mouth is stopped, I shall live with my soul. For the soul is the daughter of Love and Beauty.

I have come into this world with a purpose, to be for

everyone and with everyone. And that which I accomplish today in solitude, the masses will form into its echo Tomorrow. What is spoken today by one heart alone will be spoken Tomorrow by thousands of hearts.

Youth and Hope

Youth walked before me, and I followed it to a remote field. There it stopped and raised its eyes towards the clouds which were drifting across the sky, like a flock of sheep. Then it looked at the trees whose bare branches were stretched out towards the sky in a gesture of invocation, asking for their foliage to return.

And I said: "O Youth, to what place have we come?"

Youth replied: "To the field of confusion. Take care of yourself."

Then I cried out: "Let us leave without delay, this place frightens me."

But Youth objected: "Be patient, for it is from doubt that knowledge is born."

Then, as I looked round, I saw a graceful silhouette coming towards us. I asked: "Who is this woman?"

And Youth replied: "It is Melpomene, daughter of Zeus and Muse of Tragedy."

"But, fortunate Youth," I cried, "what can Tragedy want of me while you are beside me?"

And Youth answered me: "She has come in order to

show you the earth and its afflictions, for he who has never looked at suffering cannot claim to see joy."

Then the spirit covered my eyes with his hand. And when he withdrew it, Youth had gone. I remained alone, divested of any earthly clothing. I called out: "O you Daughter of Zeus, where then has Youth gone?"

Melpomene said not a word, but she took me under her wings and transported me to the summit of a high mountain. Below me I saw the earth and all that it contains. It lay open like the pages of a book, on which the secrets of the universe were surely printed. I remained with the young girl, full of fear, reflecting on the mystery of Man and attempting to decipher the symbols of Life.

And I saw overwhelming things.

On the earth the angels of happiness were struggling with the demons of unhappiness. Standing among them I saw Man, torn apart sometimes by hope, sometimes by despair.

I saw love and hate playing with the heart of man, love hiding from him his guilt and intoxicating him with the wine of submission, adoration, and flattery, while hate incited him to defiance, stopped his ears, and made his eyes blind to the truth.

And I saw the city crouch down over its slums and seize the clothing of Adam's son. And in the distance the compassionate fields wept over the sorrow of Man.

I saw priests with raging mouths who resembled crafty foxes, and I saw false Messiahs trying to obtain the happiness of man while conspiring against him.

And I saw preachers raise their eyes to the sky, with a gesture of adoration, while at the same time their hearts were buried deep in the tombs of greed.

I saw religion bury itself in books, and doubt rob it of its place.

And I saw man call to wisdom to aid him with deliverance and I saw wisdom show itself insensitive to his appeals, for he had looked upon it with disdain when it had spoken to him in the streets of the city.

I saw man conceal his cowardice beneath the mantle of patience, call laziness tolerance, and fear, courtesy.

And I saw a young man trying to seduce the heart of a young girl with tender words, while the true feelings of both were half asleep and they were very far from their divine nature.

I saw two lovers, and the woman seemed to be like a lute held by a man who did not know how to play it and created only discordant sounds.

And I saw lawmakers in idle discussion, selling their wares on the steps of deceit and hypocrisy.

I saw liberty walking alone and knocking on doors to ask for shelter, without anyone listening to those appeals. I saw prodigality advancing in majestic fashion and I saw the crowd acclaim it as liberty.

And I saw physicians playing with innocent and credulous souls.

I saw the ignorant man and the wise man, seated side by side, elevating their past to the throne of fame, embellishing their present with the clothing of abundance, and preparing for the future a couch of luxuriousness.

And I saw poor unfortunate men sow their fields, and the powerful reap the harvest, while oppression, disguised as the law, mounted guard.

I saw the wasteful man spend his money and the miser turn it into the fish-hook of hate. But in the hand of the Sage I saw no gold.

When I had observed all that, I cried out, heartbroken: "O daughter of Zeus, is that truly the Earth? Is that truly man?"

In a sad and subdued voice she replied: "What you have just seen is the Pathway of the Soul, paved with sharp stones and scattered with thorns. But it is only the shadow of man, the darkness. Be patient, for the morning will not be slow to come!"

Then she placed her delicate fingers over my eyes. And when she removed them I saw Youth walking slowly by my side. And, in front of us, Hope led the way.

The New Age

The world today is torn between two currents of ideas, one fixed in its past and the other aspiring to the future. And because they are lacking in strength and will, the ideas of yesterday will be vanquished forever.

On earth there is an awakening which vanquishes somnolence, an invincible awakening, for the sun is its guide and the dawn its army.

In the fields, formerly vast cemeteries, the youth of Spring calls to the ghosts of the sepulchers to rise and go forward with Time. And if the Spring does not chant its melody, then the madman of Winter will revive, rending its shroud and rising in order to go forward.

And living waves spread out into the air, rising and stretching in order to embrace the sensitive and awakened souls, to clasp the worthy and poetic hearts.

At the present time two masters inhabit this world: one commands and makes himself obeyed, even if he is a decrepit old man who is dying by the day. And the other remains silent, conforms to law and order and awaits quietly the arrival of justice, even though he is a colossus with muscular arms who, confident in his existence, knows his own strength and believes in his own values.

Nowadays, two men inhabit the earth: the man of the past and the man of the future.

Which one of them are you?

Come close so that I can look at you attentively and examine the features of your face in order to know if you are advancing towards the light or if you are sinking into darkness.

Come near and tell me who you are, what you are.

Are you the politician who says to himself: "I shall exploit my country for the sole benefit of myself?" If yes, you are a mere parasite, living on the flesh of others.

Or are you that fervent patriot whispering into the ear of his own intimate being: "I am devoting myself to my country as a faithful servant"? If yes, you are an oasis in the desert, ready to quench the thirst of the traveler.

Are you that merchant who, abusing the needs of the people, monopolizes the market in order to sell for a dinar what he bought for a piaster? If yes, you are a criminal, whether you live in a palace or a prison.

Or are you that honest and hardworking man who, as a mediator between buyer and seller, helps the weavers and the farmers in the exchange of their products, he whose fairness brings as much profit to himself as to others? If yes, you are an upright man, whether you receive praise or blame.

Are you that religious leader who weaves for his body a purple toga from the innocence of his followers and fashions a crown for his head from the simplicity of their hearts, and who, while pouring out his hatred for Satan, makes use of his riches? If yes, you are a miscreant, an atheist, even if you fast all day and pray all night long.

Or are you that pious and devoted man who sees in the virtue of the individual the foundation for the progress of a nation and in the secrets of his soul a springboard to the fulfillment of the spirit? If yes, you are a white lily in the garden of truth, may your perfume spread into the nostrils of humanity or rise freely into the upper air where the sighs of flowers are preserved.

Are you that journalist who sells his ideas and his principles in the slave market and grows fat on lies, misfortunes, and crimes, like a greedy vulture feasting on carrion? If yes, you are an open sore and an ulcer.

Or are you instead that master who stands on one of the rostra of civilization, like a preacher who, convinced of the truth of his own sermon, fills the minds of his people with the teaching inspired in him by the glories of the past? If yes, you are a panacea for suffering humanity and a balm for wounded hearts.

Are you that head of State who humbles himself before those who have named him and humbles those whom he has named, are you he who never extends his hand except to empty the purse of his subjects or to exploit them for his profit? If yes, you are only the chaff on the granary floor where the nations thresh their grain.

Or are you that faithful servant who is preoccupied with the well-being of his people and devotes himself to achieving the ambitions of the citizens? If yes, you are a blessing for their granaries.

Are you that husband who permits himself to do what he forbids to his wife, idling about and fooling while he keeps in his boots the keys to her prison, gorging on his favorite food while she remains seated in her solitude before her empty plate? If yes, you are like those savages in the past who lived in caves and concealed their nakedness beneath the skins of animals.

Or are you a companion for her, who undertakes nothing unless her hand is in his, who makes no decision without taking advice from her, and who does not succeed without making her share his joy and his ecstasy? If yes, you are like a man who, at daybreak, walks at the head of a nation, leading it to the zenith of justice, the rectitude of judgement.

Are you that writer with prying eyes who walks with his head high, dominating the crowd, while behind his eyes his thoughts stray into the gulf of past years, a gulf soiled by the rags and dross amassed down the ages? If yes, you are a stupid remark traced on paper with a few letters of the alphabet.

Or are you a limpid thought which probes its intimate being in order to teach it the art of discernment, a thought which spends its life constructing what is useful and demolishing what is dangerous? If yes, you are manna for the hungry and cool water for the thirsty.

Are you that poet who plays a tambourine at the gate of princes, who throws flowers on a wedding day, who walks in a funeral cortège and, once he arrives at the cemetery, utters hollow sounds? If yes, you are like those mountebanks who make us laugh when they cry and cry when they laugh.

Or else are you a gifted spirit in whom God has placed a viol which soothes our hearts with celestial music and makes our souls revere Life, revere everything which clothes it with beauty and makes our souls revere Life, revere everything which clothes it with beauty and magnificence? If yes, you embody a clairvoyance scintillating in our eyes, a crystalline desire in our hearts, and a divine vision in our dreams.

In this world two processions pass by: one is that of old men bowed down by age, who walk leaning on their sticks which bend beneath their weight, and although the path leads downward, they are breathless and worn out with fatigue. The other is of the procession of the young who advance with winged steps, who sing as if their throats were fitted with silver strings and who brave the obstacles which are subdued by the majesty of the mountain slopes and won over by the magic of the summits.

And you, in which procession do you take your place?

Ask yourself the question in the silence of the night. And when you finally decide to come down to earth, judge whether you are a slave of yesterday or a free man of tomorrow.

I tell you that the children of yesterday walk in the funerals of history, it has shaped them and they have shaped it themselves. They cling to a cord which has worn thin

with time; if it breaks—and this will surely happen soon—
they will fall into the depths of forgetfulness.

And I tell you that they live between crumbling walls;
as soon as the storm breaks out—and it will break out
soon—their heads will be buried beneath the rubble, and
their dwellings will be reduced to tombs.

In truth, I tell you that all they think, say, and write,
as well as their deeds, are no more than chains, and, because
they themselves are too weak, they cannot carry them, but
on the contrary it is the chains which will carry them away
by their weight.

As for the children of tomorrow, they are those who have
been summoned by life, they have followed it with a firm
step, their heads held high. They are the dawn of the New
Age. The smoke of wars will not dim their light, nor will
the clanking of their chains stifle their voices, nor will the
miasma from stagnant waters overwhelm their fragrance.

They are not very numerous among the crowd. But
they stand out like a flowering branch in a burnt-out for-
est, like a grain of wheat in a haystack. Nobody knows
them, but they know each other. They are like the moun-
tain tops which can see and hear each other, quite unlike
the caverns, which are deaf and blind.

They are the seed sown in a field by the hand of God.
It will burst forth from its husk with the strength of its
flesh, it will sway like a radiant plant facing the sun, it will
become a majestic tree, whose roots take hold in the heart
of the earth, whose branches aspire to the depths of the
firmament.

I Am Not Moderate

The extremist can equally well descend into the depths of life as he can rise up towards its heights.

The man who is moderate in his faith is the same as the man who is torn by his fear of being punished and his desire to be rewarded. And when he follows the procession of believers, he limps as he walks; and as soon as he kneels down in order to pray, his thought rises up to deride him.

The moderate suitor cannot drink from the cup of love while delighting in the freshness of its honey, nor the fire of its gall. He is content to moisten his lips on a tepid and adulterated beverage drained by stupidity from the marshes of cowardice.

The man who enjoys neither hostility to evil nor support of what is good, will not know how to destroy what evil in himself nor safeguard what is good. He limits himself to watching his life go by at the edge of the sea, like a shell, hard in appearance but soft in its inner substance, not knowing when the tide is coming in and going out.

The man who is moderate in his search for liberty will

see nothing of it beyond his footprints in the hills and valleys. For liberty is like life, it does not linger along its way to allow the disabled to catch up with it.

Moderates never stop saying: "Temperance, a cardinal virtue."

And my soul asks: "How could the monkey have become a man or the pygmy a giant by remaining moderate!"

And I have heard these monkeys and pygmies say: "Virtue stands in the middle."

So my soul moved away from them, replying: "Feeble creatures, how could you grasp the truth of all things while you keep your eyes fixed on the navel of their happy medium? Would all things then have neither tail nor head?"

And I heard those with cracked skulls repeat morning and evening: "A bird in the hand is worth two in the bush."

And my soul, livid with anger, cried out: "Those stupid people do not deserve to receive even a wing, if they do not use their feet as they run after ten birds."

Trying to catch a flock of birds: is this not our daily task, the purpose of our life, much more than life itself?

I love him who was crucified by the moderates. When he bent his head and closed his eyes, certain among them said, as though comforted: "At last this dangerous extremist is no more." Ah, if they knew that at that moment his victorious spirit was soaring over the nations and spreading out from generations to generations.

And I love those who have been sacrificed by fire, executed by the guillotine for a thought that invaded their heads and inflamed their hearts.

I love you, O extremists, you who are nourished by unfathomable ardors. Each time I raise my glass, it is your blood and your tears that I am drinking.

And each time I look through my window at the sky, it is your faces that I see.

And when a storm rises, it is your singing and your praises that I hear.

You Have Your Ideology,
I Have Mine

Your ideology is that tree rooted in the earth of habit, its branches quickened by the force of inertia.

My ideology is that cloud floating along the currents of the upper air, the cloud that lets itself fall in droplets, then drains away in a stream as far as the sea and rises again with the mist towards the heights.

Your ideology is that superannuated confession which has never evolved and which has not transformed you in any way.

Mine is a new heresy. It passes me through a strainer, and morning and evening I purify it.

Your ideology praises the union of magnificence and opulence. Mine spreads confidence in oneself.

Your ideology strives for celebrity and chases after fame. Mine deposits celebrity and fame like two grains of sand on the shore of eternity.

Your ideology consists in erecting edifices in sandalwood encrusted with jewels and decorated with plumes. Mine teaches me to have a healthy body and crystal-clear mind, even if I have no place to lay my head.

Your ideology classifies you according to your grades and your qualifications. Mine invites me to be a faithful and useful servant.

Your ideology brandishes social and religious codes as well as technical and political encyclopedias. Mine holds in its hand a few simple principles.

Mine remembers that every woman is the sister or daughter of a man, and that each man has a mother.

Your ideology punishes theft and crime, dishonesty and delinquency.

Mine tells you that the assassin is the ally of the victim, the thief is the reject of the miser, and that dishonesty and marginality are no different from a display of vainglory and an excess of firmness.

Your ideology speaks of Judaism, Brahmanism, Buddhism, Christianity, and Islam.

Mine reveals to you that there is no confession other than absolute religion which has many aspects and many paths, but remains always unique, like a single hand which opens out into five fingers.

Your ideology classifies the rich and the poor, he who gives and he who receives. Mine cries out: "We are all poor, and nobody is rich except Life. We all receive, and nobody gives except Life."

Your ideology claims that nations are evaluated according to their politics, their parties, and their congresses, and in accordance with their decisions and their pacts.

Mine decrees that the only merit of a nation is the labor

of each one of its citizens.

Your ideology believes that the fame of a people is due to their conquering heroes. And it swells with pride when mentioning Nebuchadnezzar, Ramses, Alexander, Caesar, Hannibal, and Napoleon.

Mine sees heroism in the works of Confucius, Lao Tzu, Socrates, and Plato, as well as Ali, Ghazali, and Rumi, without forgetting Copernicus and Pasteur.

Your ideology attributes the greatness of a State to the exhaustiveness of its troops at war, the efficacy of its satanic arsenal, and the ingeniousness of its chemical weapons.

Mine stipulates that there is no superiority wherever rectitude is thrust aside, and that there is no will if it does not support truth. The longer the victory of muscles swollen with technical prowess lasts, the more sudden will be their ruin.

You have your ideology, I have mine.

Your ideology is that which enjoys the protection of the coterie or the pleasures of life.

My ideology is the thought of every wanderer in his own country, and the feeling of every stranger in the country where he lives.

You Have Your Lebanon, I Have Mine

You have your Lebanon with its dilemma. I have my Lebanon with its beauty.

You have your Lebanon with all the conflicts that rage there. I have my Lebanon with the dreams that live there.

You have your Lebanon, accept it. I have my Lebanon and I accept nothing other than the absolute abstract.

Your Lebanon is a political knot which the years attempt to untie. My Lebanon is made up of hills which rise with great presence and magnificence towards the azure sky.

Your Lebanon is an international problem beset with the shadows of night. My Lebanon is made up of silent and mysterious valleys whose slopes gather together the sound of bells and the trickling of streams.

Your Lebanon is a tilting ground where men from the West struggle with others from the South. My Lebanon is a winged prayer which hovers at morning, when the shepherds lead their flocks to pasture, and flies away at evening, when the peasants return from their fields and their vines.

Your Lebanon is an octopus-government with numerous tentacles. My Lebanon is a tranquil and revered hill, set between seas and plains, like a poet halfway between Creation and Eternity.

Your Lebanon is a ruse devised by the fox when he encounters the hyena and the latter plots against the wolf. My Lebanon is made up of memories which recall to me the humming of young girls on nights of the full moon, and the songs of little girls between the threshing floor and the wine-press.

Your Lebanon is a chessboard set between a religious leader and a military leader. My Lebanon is a temple which I visit within my spirit, when my gaze wearies of the face of this civilization which advances on wheels.

Your Lebanon is one man who pays tribute and another who collects taxes. My Lebanon is one man only, his head leaning on his arm, relaxing in the shade of the Cedar, forgetful of everything, except God and the light of the sun.

Your Lebanon lives on ships and trade. My Lebanon is a distant thought, an ardent desire, and a noble word whispered by the earth into the ear of the universe.

Your Lebanon is made up of clerks, workers, and directors. My Lebanon is the valour of youth, the power of middle age, and the wisdom of the old.

Your Lebanon is made up of delegations and committees. My Lebanon is made up of winter evenings warmed by the fire in the hearth, draped in the majesty of storms, and embroidered by the purity of the snows.

Your Lebanon is a country of speeches and disputes.

My Lebanon is a twittering of blackbirds, a rustling of oaks and poplars. It is the echo of lutes in grottoes and caverns.

Your Lebanon is no more than deceit hiding behind borrowed erudition, hypocrisy concealed by mannerisms and playacting. My Lebanon is simple, naked truth; since it is reflected in the pool round a fountain, it sees only its serene and happy face.

Your Lebanon is made up of laws and clauses on paper, treaties and pacts in registers. My Lebanon is innate but unconscious knowledge, a knowledge inborn in the mysteries of life, and a desire that is awake, touching lightly the fringes of the invisible, believing that it is dreaming.

Your Lebanon is an old man who, fingering his beard and knitting his brows, thinks only of himself. My Lebanon is a young man who stands up like a fortress, smiles like the dawn, and is aware of other people as of his intimate being.

Your Lebanon sometimes detaches itself from Syria, sometimes attaches itself again; it cheats on both sides and finishes between the two of them. My Lebanon neither detaches nor attaches itself, and knows neither conquest nor defeat.

You have your Lebanon, I have mine.

You may have your Lebanon and its children, I shall have mine and its children.

And who are the children of your Lebanon?

Let the scales fall from your eyes so that I can show you the reality of your children.

They are those who saw their souls born in Western hospitals.

They are those who saw their minds awaken in the arms of a miser who feigns munificence.

They are those pliable rods which bend here and there involuntarily, which quiver morning and evening without knowing it.

They are that ship which, without sail or rudder, attempts to brave a raging sea while her captain is none other than a cave full of ogres. And would not each European capital have been a cave full of ogres?

Between themselves they are strong and eloquent. But faced with the Europeans they are impotent and speechless.

In their pulpits and their newspapers they are liberal, reforming, and fiery. But in front of Westerners they are docile and retarded.

They are those who croak like frogs as they boast that they have escaped from their ancient and tyrannical enemy, but he remains buried in their flesh.

They are those who join a funeral cortège, singing and dancing, and if they pass a wedding procession, their chanting will turn into lamentation and their dance into open repentance.

They are those who are unaware of famine unless it robs their pockets. And if they meet someone whose spirit is hungry they will laugh at him and avoid him, treating him like a shadow wandering through the world of shadows.

They are those slaves whose rusty chains have become polished with time and who believe they have been really freed.

Such are the children of your Lebanon!

Who among them would represent the power of the Lebanese rocks, the nobility of its heights, the crystal of its waters, and the fragrance of its air?

Which one among them would say: "When I die, I shall have left my country slightly better than it was at my birth"?

Is there a single one among them who would dare to say: "Indeed, my life was a drop of blood in the veins of the Lebanon, a tear in its eyes, or a smile on its lips"?

Such are the children of your Lebanon!

How great they seem in your eyes, and how minute in mine.

Stop for a moment and open your eyes wide so that I can unveil to you the reality of the children of my Lebanon.

They are those tillers of the soil who transform arid lands into gardens and orchards.

They are those shepherds who lead their flocks from one valley to another so that they will grow fat and multiply, until their flesh will furnish your table and their wool will clothe your body.

They are those vinegrowers who crush the grapes to make them into wine and draw off the grape jelly.

They are those fathers who tend the mulberry trees and those mothers who spin the silken thread.

They are those men who harvest the wheat, whose wives gather it up in armfuls.

They are those poets who pour their souls into new goblets, those innate poets who sing laments and Levantine love-songs.

They are those who leave the Lebanon in their destitute state, they have only fire in their hearts and strength in their arms. And when they return, their hands are brimming with the riches of the earth and their heads are crowned with laurel.

They are conquerors wherever they settle, and charmers wherever they are.

They are those who are born in cottages and die in the places of knowledge.

Such are the children of my Lebanon.

They are those torches which defy the wind and that salt which disarms time.

They are those who advance with a firm step towards truth, beauty, and fulfillment.

What could possible remain of your Lebanon and its children at the end of the century?

Tell me, what will you bequeath to that future beyond aggressive men, fantasists and failures?

Do you hope that time holds in its memory the traces of your sly evasions, your cheating, and your trickery?

Do you believe that the upper air absorbs the shadows of death and the fetid exhalations from the tombs?

Do you still cherish the illusion which claims that life clothes its naked body with rags?

I tell you this, and truth is my witness.

The smallest olive seedling planted by a villager at the foot of Mount Lebanon will outlive all your deeds and exploits. And the ploughshare and the plough drawn by the oxen on the Lebanese slopes are more worthy and more dignified than your combined dreams and ambitions.

I tell you this, and the conscience of the universe heeds me.

The song of a little girl gathering flowers in the valleys of the Lebanon will live longer than the statements of the most powerful and the most eminent talk among you.

I tell you this, you are worthless. And if you knew it, my disgust for you would be transformed into pity and tenderness. But you know nothing of it at all.

You have your Lebanon, I have mine.

You have your Lebanon and its children, so be satisfied with that. Ah, if only you succeed in convincing your relatives that it is all as empty as a bubble of air!

As for me, I am convinced about my Lebanon and its children, and in my conviction there reign freshness silence and tranquility.

Life

Life is like an island lost in the ocean of solitude, an island where the rocks are our hopes and the trees our dreams, where the flowers are our solitude and the streams our aspirations.

Your Life is an island separate from all the other islands and regions. However many vessels leave your shores for other countries, however many fleets sail to your ports, you will always be a separate island, suffering the pangs of solitude and aspiring to happiness. Other men do not know you at all and they are far from pitying your solitude or understanding you.

My brother, your life is like an isolated house, far from any human dwelling. A house which no gaze from outside can penetrate.

If it were deprived of light your neighbor's lamp could not illuminate it. If the house stood in the desert you could not transport it into the garden of other men, ploughed and cultivated by other hands.

My brother, the life of the spirit goes by in solitude, and without this solitude and this isolation you would be in no way what you are, neither would I be what I am. Without this isolation and this solitude, I should come to believe on hearing your voice that it is my voice which is speaking, or on seeing your face that it is the reflection of my face in a mirror.

❧

Life without rebellion is like the seasons without spring.

And rebellion without rights is like spring in a barren desert.

Life, rebellion, and right are a trinity which can neither be changed nor separated.

Life is like the charger of the night: the faster it gallops the sooner will come the dawn.

Yesterday, Today, and Tomorrow

I said to my friend, "Look at that woman sitting so close to that man, while yesterday she was leaning on my arm."

And my friend added, "And tomorrow it will be my arm."

I said, "See how she drinks from that man's glass, while only yesterday she was getting drunk on my wine."

And my friend added, "And tomorrow it will be my goblet."

I said, "See, how she looks at him tenderly. And yesterday her glance was caressing my eyes."

And my friend added, "And tomorrow it will be my eyes."

I said, "Listen to her whispering. And yesterday she was murmuring to me the sweetest of words."

And my friend added, "And tomorrow they will be spoken into my ear."

I said, "Look, she is embracing him. Yesterday she was burying her face against my chest."

And my friend added, "And tomorrow it will be against mine."

Then I said, "What a strange woman!"
And my friend revealed to me: "She is like life.
She is possessed by all men, like life.
She conquers all men, like death.
She broods over all men, like eternity."

Woman-Life

The woman whom I loved is like that woman who caused your heart to throb.

She is so astonishingly beautiful that you might think she was the handiwork of the gods.

She was fashioned with the gentleness of the dove, the evasiveness of serpents, the vanity of the peacock, and the cruelty of the wolf.

She was modeled with the magnificent alabaster of the lily and the terrifying ebony of the night.

He body is a handful of ashes and a cupful of froth.

I knew that woman in my childhood. I used to run with her across the fields and vineyards, and going through the market I would grasp the fringes of her dress.

I knew that woman during my youth. I would see the shadow of her face on the pages of books and in the verses of the Scriptures.

And I knew her during my middle-age. I exchanged words and counsel with her and, sitting close to her, I opened my heart and poured out my soul.

To her I confided the problems of my heart and bared the secrets of my soul.

My true love is called Life.

Life is a woman of intoxicating beauty.

She bewitches our hearts and seduces our souls.

She consumes our consciences in her promises.

And if she keeps them, she awakens boredom within us. And if she lingers over them, she kills patience within us.

Life is a woman who purifies herself in the tears of her suitors and anoints her body with the blood of her victims.

She clothes herself in the brightness of day, and her garment is lined with the darkness of night.

She falls in love with the heart of man in its early gleaming moments and forgets herself in marriage.

Life is an enchantress, and her graces seduce us, but anyone who knows her guile will flee her charms.

Woman

I owe Woman all my life,
I owe her this self which was born from a cry,
I owe her all my writing.

Woman opened my eyes.
Woman freed my soul.

Without Woman-mother,
Woman-sister, and Woman-friend,
I should have dozed among those for whom
Drowsiness is a divinity
And snoring a form of worship.

On Woman

Writers and poets try to understand the truth about woman, but until today they have never understood her heart.

For they look at her through the veil of desire and see only the shape of her body.

And they look at her through the magnifying glass of self-love and find in her only weakness and submission.

The woman of yesterday was a happy woman, but the woman of today is a wretched mistress.

In the past she walked blindly in the light. But now she walks with her eyes wide open in the darkness. Nowadays she has become ugly in her spontaneity, superficial and heartless in her knowledge.

Will the day come when men will allow beauty, understanding, innocence, and virtue, the weakness of the body and the strength of the soul, to lodge within woman?

Remembrance of My Youth

Remembering the dawn of your youth pours a balm of happiness over your heart, although you regret the flight of those happy days.

As for myself, I remember it as a liberated slave cherishes the recollection of his prison walls and the links of his chains.

You speak of those years which stretch between childhood and youth like a golden age that laughs at the torments of life and the turning points of destiny, an age that surmounts without concern labors and misfortunes, as the bee crosses stagnant marshes in order to fly away towards gardens full of flowers.

My youth was full of mysterious and silent sorrows which lodged in my heart, they rebelled stormily in my veins and magnified throughout my adolescence

And my sorrows found no solution in the world of Understanding until the day when my love opened the lock-gates of my heart and illuminated its dreams.

Love freed my tongue, and I spoke.

It opened my eyes, and I wept.

It loosened my throat, and I sighed.

You remember the fields, the gardens, and the public places, as well as the street corners which observed your eyes and your innocent whisperings.

I too, I remember a wonderful place in north Lebanon. As soon as I close my eyes on my surroundings, wherever I am, I see again those valleys full of flowers, full of secrets and dignity, those high mountains whose majesty seems to reach the sky.

And as soon as I shut myself up into silence far from the clamor of civilizations, I hear the murmur of the streams and the rustles of the branches.

I yearn to see again all those beauties I am describing to you, as a newborn baby demands its mother's breast.

I suffered as a falcon suffers behind the bars of his cage when he catches sight of other falcons soaring happily over the vast horizon.

This same painful nostalgia took over my being during those moments of meditation and contemplation, hanging a veil of hopelessness over my heart.

I never went into the countryside without returning sad and I never knew the causes of this sadness.

I never looked at the sunset obscured by clouds without feeling the hurt of a broken heart. Even the twittering of birds and the music of the streams made me suffer, and I could not understand the reason for this unhappiness.

It is said that ignorance is the cradle of nothingness and that nothingness is the seat of unconcern.

That is only true in the case of those who exist on earth like bodies without life.

If this ignorance is increased by a fair and awakened sensitivity, it becomes more bitter than death. For a young emotional person, who feels intensely but knows little, is the most unhappy creature on earth.

He finds himself torn between two forces: an invisible force which uplifts him and shows him the beauty of existence through a mist of dreams, and a visible force which binds him to the earth, fills his eyes with dust, subjects him to fear, and leads him astray in the darkness.

Melancholy has a silken hand, but its grip is powerful It takes hold of the heart and afflicts it in solitude.

And this solitude, allied with melancholy, is also the companion of all spiritual exaltation.

When the soul of a young man is possessed by melancholy and solitude, it resembles a lily that is barely in flower.

It trembles in the wind, opens its corolla at dawn and closes it at nightfall.

But if this young man has no distractions to occupy his mind or companions to share his games, life will appear to him like a cramped prison where he will see only spiders' webs and hear only the muffled movements of insects.

Now, at this period, I could have entertainments and I knew where to find friends.

However, melancholy alone obsessed my heart.

It killed within me the wish to play games.

It tore from me the wings of youth and transformed my being into a pool where the water reflected the shadow of spirits, the color of clouds and the outline of branches, without ever finding a way out which would allow it to run singing towards the sea.

That was my life until the age of eighteen.

That year of my past placed me on a mountaintop, and as I looked at the world I questioned humanity about its aspirations, its efforts, and its struggles, while I tried to understand its laws and its customs.

That year I was born anew.

For anyone whose youth is not the embryo of his sadness, whose despair is not the child of his sorrows, whose love is not the cradle of his dreams, will imagine his whole life as a blank page in the book of existence.

That year I was born a second time through the eyes of a beloved woman, whose beauty was total and complete.

And through the eyes of that sublime woman the angels looked at me and at the same time I saw the angels of hell squirming and shouting in the hearts of a criminal man.

He who does not see those angels and demons through the joys and vicissitudes of life will leave his mind denuded of feeling and his heart far removed from understanding.

Here Lies My First Love

One day love, with its magic rays of light, opened my eyes, and for the first time it lightly touched my soul with its fingers of fire.

I was eighteen years old!

Through her charm, the first woman in my life awakened my spirit and began to walk before me in that Eden of sublime feelings, when days evaporate like dreams and nights die down like wedding feasts.

Through her beauty she taught me the cult of the beautiful.

Through her grace she revealed to me the secrets of love.

And through her voice, the first line from the poem of inner life caressed my hearing.

What man does not remember the first girl who through her gentleness and purity transformed the indolence of his youth into an awakening that was remarkable, poignant, and destructive?

What man would not be consumed with nostalgia at the memory of that strange moment?

Who would refuse to see his being overturned and transformed and his innermost organs grow farther apart, stretch out, and become filled with delectable reactions, despite the bitterness produced by modesty, while they are also filled with feelings of pleasure despite so many tears, desires, and nights of insomnia.

My life was like a desert, as though paralyzed, like the sleep of Adam in paradise, until the day when that woman rose up before me, like a pillar of light.

She became the Eve of that heart which was filled with mysteries and marvels.

And it was she who caused it to grasp the quintessence of existence and led it to mirror within itself ecstasies and hallucinations.

The first strong-willed Eve dragged the acquiescent Adam out of paradise while my first Eve, through her gentleness and benevolence, drew me into the Eden of love and purity.

Yet what happened to Adam happened to me.

The sword of fire which drove the first man out of paradise was like that sword which frightened me through the brightness of its blade and cast me out of the paradise of love before I broke any commandment, before I tasted the fruit of good and evil.

And my Eve was relegated beyond the azure sky, leaving behind her two tombs, her own in the shadow of the cedars of Beirut and my heart buried by sighs. Neither the silence of her tomb nor the roots in the earth will be able to bring our divine secret to light.

Only my heart which, in pouring out its black ink, can light up the scene of this tragedy in which the heroes are love, beauty, and death.

O young people of Beirut, I beg you to visit this mausoleum with muffled steps, to take a handful of the earth which embraces her body and evoke my name, saying:

"Here lie the hopes of this man.

Here begins the exile of his heart."

O God of Love, of Life and Death!

You who are the creator of our souls, who guides our minds as much towards the light as towards the darkness, who soothes our hearts and stimulates them through hope and suffering, you have torn me away from my country and established me in another; you have revealed to me the supremacy of death over life and sorrow over joy.

You have planted a white lily in the desert of my broken heart. Then you took me away to a distant valley, and there you showed me a lily that had faded.

In telling this story my intention is not to complain, for he who complains is doubtful about Life. Now my faith in Life is unshakable.

I think it is good that bitterness is mixed into every mouthful that I drink from the cup of Life.

I believe in the beauty of sadness filling my heart, but also in the ultimate mercy of the fingers of steel which clasp my soul.

I regret nothing of my years in exile. For he who seeks truth and tells it to humanity must expect to suffer. My sorrows have taught me to understand those of others.

O young people of Beirut, I entreat you to place a flower on her forgotten tomb, just as the eyes of dawn let fall a drop of dew on the petals of a shriveled rose.

The Mystery of Love

Yesterday I found myself on the steps of the Temple questioning passers-by about the mysteries and merits of Love.

An old man with a worn and melancholy face replied to me: "Love is a natural weakness which was bequeathed to us by the first man."

And a healthy young man said to me: "Love links our present to the roots of our past and to the dome of our future."

Then there came a woman with a tragic face who told me with a sigh: "Love is a mortal poison injected by black vipers from the caverns of hell.

"This poison seems as cool as the dew and the thirsty soul drinks great mouthfuls of it. But once he is intoxicated with it the drinker will be overcome with languors and will die a painful death."

And a young girl with rosy cheeks and joyful eyes replied to me: "Love is wine served by the betrothed of the dawn. It strengthens firm souls and allows them to rise up to the stars."

Then I questioned two bearded men wearing black

robes. One told me, knitting his brows: "Love is the blind ignorance in which youth begins and ends."

And the other, with a smile on his lips, replied: "Love is a divine knowledge which allows man to see what the gods see."

Then a blind man seeking his way with the tip of his cane said to me: "Love is a blinding fog which prevents the soul from discerning the secret of existence, in such a way that the heart no longer sees in the hills anything more than the trembling phantoms of desire and no longer hears anything beyond the echoes of weeping from the silent valleys."

And a decrepit old man said to me in a quavering voice: "Love is the repose of the body in the silences of the tomb, the tranquility of the soul, and the depths of eternity."

And a child of five accompanied by his parents said to me, laughingly, "Love is my father and my mother, and they are the only ones who know what it is."

And so each passer-by evoked love as the reflection of his hopes and frustrations; and the mystery still remained obscure.

Love

Love is the only seed that grows and flowers without the help of the sections.

Love is the only freedom that exists in the world, for it lifts the spirit so high that men and the phenomena of nature cannot change its course.

Men and women can only find love after a sad and revealing separation, bitter patience, and desperate efforts.

When we lose a friend we are comforted and consoled by seeing around us those who remain.

When we lose our fortune we think about it for a time. Then, knowing that the efforts which assured us of opulence will return to assist us, we forget it.

But if we lose a love, where can we go to seek peace of mind?

The ardors of the heart spread out like the branches of the cedar.

If the love-tree loses a branch, it will certainly suffer, but it will not die as a result. Instead it will breathe all its vitality into the neighboring branch which will grow larger to fill the empty place.

Oh how wretched is the man who suddenly learns that his beloved wife, whose heart he had been trying to buy, through work by day and vigilance by night, has offered her intimate secrets and her ardent love to another, who thus knows happiness.

Oh how wretched is the woman who awakens at the end of her careless youth and sees her husband grant her all the honors and advantages of a sumptuous life, without, alas, filling her head with the immortal draught of love for which she yearns.

A limited love wants to possess the beloved being, but he whose self is a vast ocean only seeks his own shores.

Those who have not been chosen by love as its disciples cannot hear its appeals.

Hell lies not in torture.
Hell lies in an empty heart.

The First Glance

It is the moment which separates the intoxication of life and its awakening, the first gleam of light which illuminates the intimate regions of the soul, the first magic note played on the silver string of our heart.

The first glance is the fleeting moment which destroys before the soul the chronicles of time, which reveals to the eye the actions of the night and the working of the conscience. This moment unveils to the future the secrets of Eternity. It is like the seed broadcast by Ishtar, the goddess of love, and sown by the eyes of the beloved in the field of love, seed germinated by tenderness and ripened by the Soul.

The first glance from the beloved is like that spirit which floated over the waves, creating heaven and earth when the Lord pronounced those words: "Let there be ... "

The First Kiss

It is the first drop drunk from the cup that is filled with the nectar of life.

It is the line which divides doubt, deceiving the mind and saddening the soul, and the certainty which floods the intimate being with joy.

It is the link that connects the obscurity of the past to the bright light of the future, the link between the silence of feelings and their melody.

It is the first line of the song of life.

It is the word pronounced together by four lips, which makes the heart into a throne, love into a king, and fidelity into a crown.

The first kiss is the light touch on the lips of the rose by the delicate fingers of the breeze, when you can hear the rose utter a long sigh of relief and a gentle moan.

It is the union of two scented flowers, so that their mingled perfumes can summon the bee to gather its nectar.

With the first kiss is born that magic vibration that will transport the lovers from the measurable world into the world of dreams and revelations.

Just as the first glance is like a seed sown by the goddess in the field of the human heart, the first kiss is the first flower which blooms at the tip of the branch of the Tree of Life.

Marriage

With marriage love begins to transform the prose of life into hymns and canticles of praise.

With marriage, aspiration to love throws back its veil and lights up the depths of the heart; it creates a happiness that no other happiness could possibly surpass, except for that of the soul embracing God.

Marriage is the union of two divinities, allowing a third one to be born on earth. Marriage leads to that superior unity in which two distinct incarnated minds are fused into two separate individualities.

It is the gold ring in a chain which began by a glance and will end in Eternity. It is rain falling from a clear sky to enrich and bless the fields of divine Nature.

In the same way that the first glance at the beloved is like the seed scattered in the heart of man, and in the same way that the first kiss bestowed on her lips is like a flower on the branch of the Tree of Life, the union of two lovers in marriage is like the first fruit of the first flower from that seed.

Children

The flowers of the fields are the children of sunshine and nature.

The children of men are the flowers of love and compassion.

Mother

The mother is everything in life.

She is the consolation in our sadness, the hope in our distress, the strength in our weakness.

She is the source of compassion, she is love and grace.

He who loses his mother loses a breast on which to lay his head, a hand that blesses him, a gaze that protects him.

Other People

Through defending yourself you have finally become full of hate.

If you were stronger, you would not use such weapon.

He who understands you is closer to you than your own brother.

For it can happen that even your parents are unable either to grasp the secret of your heart or to appreciate your true worth.

Giving

The coin that you place in the hand that inspires pity is the only chain of gold that links the humanity within you to the heart of the Divine.

Riches and Poverty

How long will the people remain asleep?

How long will they glorify those who only acquired greatness by luck?

How long will they remain unaware of those who allowed them to see the beauty of their spirit, the symbol of peace and love?

How long will men honor the dead while remaining unaware of those who spend their lives in a circle of poverty, who consume themselves like burning candles in order to light up the road for those who are unaware and lead them to the pathways of light?

My Friend, the Dispossessed

If you could know that the poverty which causes so many ravages is the same poverty that reveals the knowledge of justice and the understanding of life, you would be satisfied with your lot.

I say knowledge of justice, for the rich are occupied in amassing riches, so much so that they have no time to seek this knowledge.

And I say understanding of life, for powerful people yearn to acquire power and fame, so much so that they cannot remain on the direct path to truth.

Hope is full of promise for the future.

Remember that divinity is the true nature of man. It cannot be exchanged for gold, nor accumulated like the riches of the present world.

The power that you sow for the rich, you will harvest in the future. For the laws of nature mean that every thing returns to its source.

And by means of suffering and poverty, the generations of tomorrow will receive a lesson from Love and Equality.

The Law of Man

Are you one of those born in the cradle of suffering, and then brought up in the lap of ill-fortune or in the house of oppression?

Do you eat crusts of bread moistened by your tears? Do you drink clouded water in which blood is mingled with tears?

Are you that young woman who, having received beauty from God, has become prey to the base greed of the rich, who have deceived you by buying your body but not your soul, while abandoning you to poverty and distress?

If your answer is yes, you are a martyr to the law of man.

You are like the bare tree which bends beneath the weight of snow in winter. But spring will come and throw its mantle of green over you. And Truth will rend the veil of tears which hides your smile.

Beyond our material world resides a vast power, a power which is solely justice, compassion, and love.

Courage

Courage is a volcano.
   The seed of indecision never grows in its center.

Braving the miseries of life is more noble than shutting yourself up in silence.
   The moth that flutters round the fire until its own death is more admirable than the mole who lives in a dark tunnel.

The Law

What is the law?

Who saw it come with the sun from the uttermost depths of heaven?

What man has seen the heart of God and understood His will or His plans?

In what century did the angels walk among the people and preach, saying:

"Forbid the weak to enjoy life, kill the outlaws with the edge of the sword, and trample on sinners with feet of bronze"?

The Worship of Slavery

I have been present in remote ages, from the banks of the Ganges to the edge of the Euphrates, from the delta of the Nile to the plains of Assyria, from the theaters of Athens to the churches of Rome, from the hovels of Constantinople to the palaces of Alexandria.

And yet everywhere I have seen slavery pass by in a glorious and majestic procession of ignorance.

I have seen nations sacrifice boys and girls at the feet of the idol they call God, burn incense before his statue, calling it Son of God, I have seen them submit to its will, calling it the Shadow of God on earth, I have seen them pour over it wine and perfume, calling it Queen, worshipping it and kneeling before it, calling it Law, working and fighting, even stealing for it, calling it Good Fortune and Happiness, fighting and dying for it, calling that Patriotism, destroying and demolishing in its name, calling that Fraternity, and finally killing for it, calling that Equality.

Numerous are the names of this idol, but the reality is

unique. It has several facets, but it consists of one element only.

In fact it is a perpetual malady, transmitted from generation to generation.

War

What is peace? Is it found in the eyes of those children who are fed from the withered breasts of their mothers, in icy cold huts?

Or is it in the ruined shacks of hungry people who sleep on the dunes and long for a single mouthful of that food which priests and pastors distribute to their fat pigs?

Are you that soldier constrained by harsh human law to abandon wife and children to advance towards the field of battle in the name of Greed, which your leaders wrongfully call Duty?

What is this duty that separates lovers, turns women into widows and children into orphans?

What is this patriotism that provokes wars and destroys kingdoms over trifles?

What is this duty that drags poor villagers, who are treated as less than nothing by the rich citizens and the children of hereditary nobility, to die for the glory of their oppressors?

If duty destroys peace among nations, if patriotism disturbs the peace of a citizen's life, let us say then: "Let duty and patriotism rest in peace!"

❧

You are my brother, but why do you quarrel with me? Why do you invade my country and try to subjugate me in order to please those who seek fame and authority?

Why do you leave your wife and children and follow death as far as that distant country on behalf of those who buy their glory with your blood and their honor with the tears of your mother?

Is it an honor for a man to kill his brother? If you believe that, make it into an act of worship and build a temple to Cain who killed his brother Abel.

Liberty

Liberty invites us to her table to savor the delicious food and heady wines she offers. But since we are her guests we eat voraciously and try to gorge ourselves.

I am told: "If you see a slave sleeping, do not be afraid to wake him. He may be dreaming of liberty."

I reply: "If you see a slave sleeping, wake him and teach him what liberty is."

To die for liberty is more noble than living in the shadow of cowardly submission.

For he who embraces death with the sword of truth in his hand will live forever in eternity and truth.

Life is weaker than death, and death is weaker than truth.

The Children of Liberty

During a night of the full moon I was walking alone in the valley of the shadows of life.

And then a pallid phantom, gazing at the moon, collapsed at my feet.

And in a frightened voice I asked him: "Who are you?"

"I am liberty, near death," he told me.

And I asked him: "Is it your last wish to see your children?"

And liberty replied in tears:

"One died on the cross, the other died mad, and the third is not yet born."

Truth

Truth is like the stars: it shows only in the darkness of the night.

Truth is like all the beautiful things in this world: it reveals its attractiveness only to those who have first felt the influence of falsehood.

A truth which needs to be proved is a half-truth.

Ignorance

In the house of ignorance there is no mirror in which to contemplate your soul.

If you cannot discern the mote in your own eye, you will surely not notice it in your neighbor's.

Friendliness with an ignorant man is just as absurd as discussion with a drunkard.

When the tide was coming in I traced some wise words on the sand by the sea, and wagered my reason on them, adding my entire soul.

When the tide had gone out, I retraced my steps to decipher and demystify what was there; alas, in the memory of the beaches I found only my own ignorance!

Teaching and Knowledge

Before teaching others begin by educating yourselves. Teach by example before teaching by words.

Knowledge makes your seeds germinate but never sows them.

Understanding

The merit of a man lies in his understanding and in his deeds, not at all in the color of his skin or in what he believes.

Understanding forms the only set of riches which tyrants cannot take away from you.

The true riches of a nation lie not in its gold or silver but in its aptitude to educate itself and in the degree of integrity possessed by its children.

The riches of the mind embellish the face of a man and earn sympathy and respect. The mind of a being is reflected in his eyes and in all the movements and gestures of his body.

Reason and Understanding

When reason speaks to you, listen to what it says and you shall be saved. Make good use of its words and you shall be armed. For reason is a clever minister, a loyal guide, and a wise counselor. And just as anger obscures the light, reason is a light in the darkness.

Do not forget, however, that even if reason illuminates you, it is not effective without understanding. Without its true-born sister, reason is a wanderer without a roof over its head; and understanding without reason is like an unguarded house.

Reason and understanding are not like the merchandise that is sold in the market, whose value goes down with abundance; quite the contrary, the more abundant they are, the more their value increases.

Joy and Sorrow

Joy is a myth that we seek. And when we find joy, it angers us, just as the river which hastens towards the plain slows down and darkens when it arrives there.

For men are only happy through their aspiration to the heights. And when they achieve their aim, they become disillusioned and aspire to other, longer journeys.

I would not exchange the laughter in my heart for the fortune of the multitudes.

And I should feel no satisfaction if the tears shed in the agony of my being were transformed into relief.

My most fervent hope is that my entire life on this earth should consist of laughter and tears.

Pain

At the heart of every winter, there is a quivering spring;
and behind the veil of each night there is a smiling dawn.

The Body and the Mind

He who tries to separate the body from the mind or the mind from the body distances his heart from the truth.

For the flower and its perfume are inseparable.

And the blind man who denies the colors and contours of the flower, believing that it possesses only a perfume that vibrates in the upper air, is like the man who pinches his nostrils and claims that flowers are only shapes and colors without any scent.

Life is naked.

And a naked body represents the truest and most noble symbol of life.

And if I draw a mountain as a heap of human forms, if I paint a waterfall as a cascade of falling naked bodies, it is because I see in a mountain a mass of living things, and in a waterfall a current of rushing life.

The body is the bosom where the soul takes up residence until it is mature.

It rises then in order to soar upwards, while the womb opens to accept a new seed.

The Mind

The mind manifests itself by looks and words.

For the soul is our dwelling-place, our eyes are its windows, and our lips its messengers.

The mere strength of the mind is more powerful than all powers, and must sometimes grind to dust everything that opposes it.

However, have pity on men of little faith.

Have pity on their weakness, their ignorance, and their nothingness.

Unity

The stone concealed in the heart of the ripe date has been the secret of the palm tree ever since the dawn of Creation.

Everything that is in creation exists within you, and everything that exists within you exists in creation.

There is no frontier between you and the things that are closest, nor any distance between you and the things that are farthest away.

And all things, from the lowest to the highest, from the smallest to the greatest, are within you in perfectly equal parts.

In an atom you find all the elements of the earth; in a motion of the spirit are all the motions of the laws of existence; in a drop of water are all the secrets of the boundless oceans.

And in one aspect of you are all the aspects of existence.

From the Pygmy-Self
to the Giant-Self

In the depths of the soul there is a profound desire which draws man from the visible to the invisible, to philosophy and the divine.

You are all fragile and without firm shape, but you are the roots of giant oak trees and an outline sketch of willows on the canvas of the sky.

Our self is constantly on a pilgrimage to the Holy City.

What Are You and Who Are You, Earth?

Are you that speck of dust raised by the footsteps of God when he left the East of the universe to go to the West of the firmament, or are you that glowing spark in the hearth of Eternity?

Are you that seed cast into the fields of the upper air, tearing apart the husk with the urging of its flesh, the seed that would grow into a divine tree above the layers of atmosphere in the ether?

Are you that drop of blood in the veins of the Lord of the Giants, or that bead of sweat on his brow?

Are you that fruit cherished by the sun? Do you live on the tree of universal knowledge whose roots extend from the depths of Creation, while its branches stretch up to the heights of Eternity?

Or are you that wedding ring placed by the god of time on the finger of the goddess of space?

Who are you, Earth, and what are you?

You are my sight and my clairvoyance. You are my reflections and my imaginings, my hunger and my thirst, my grief and my joy, my sleep and my awakening.

You are the beauty in my eyes, the ardor in my heart, the Eternity in my spirit.

You are me, O Earth!

If I did not exist, you would never be there.

And if you had not existed, you would have had to be invented.

Earth

How beautiful you are, Earth, and how sublime!

What wisdom in your obedience to the light, and what nobility in your submission to the sun!

How seductive you are when veiled in shadow and how radiant is your face beneath the mask of darkness!

How crystalline are your songs at dawn and how marvelous are the praises sung at the hour of your twilight!

How perfect you are, Earth, and how majestic!

I have crossed your plains and climbed your mountains; I have gone down into your valleys and entered your caves.

On the plains I have discovered your dreams; on the mountains I have admired your splendid presence.

And in the valleys I have observed your tranquility; among the rocks I have felt your firmness; in the caves I have touched your mysteries.

You who are relaxed in your strength, haughty in your modesty, humble in your arrogance, gentle in your resistance, limpid in your secrets.

I have crossed your seas, explored your rivers, and walked the banks of your streams.

I have heard Eternity speak through your ebb and flow and the ages return the echoes of your melodies over your hillsides.

And I have heard Life calling to itself in your mountain passes and along your valley slopes.

You are the tongue and lips of Eternity, the cords and fingers of Eternity, the thoughts and words of Life.

Your Spring awoke me and led me towards your forests, where your breathing exhales in the distance its sweet perfume in spirals of incense.

Your Summer invited me into your fields to be present at your labor, at the birth of your jewel-like fruits.

Your Autumn showed me, in your vineyards, your blood running like wine.

Your Winter took me into its bed where your purity broadcasts its flakes of snow.

You are fragrance when young, force when growing, magnificence in middle life, and with the ice of old age, you are crystal.

On a starry night I opened the lock-gates of my soul and went out to be at your side, with a curious and hungry heart. And I saw you looking at the stars which were smiling at you.

Then I cast off my chains and shackles, for I discovered that the lodging of the soul is your universe, that its desires grow within yours, that its peace dwells within your peace, and that its joy lies in that long hair of stars that the night spreads over your body.

One misty night, weary of idle dreaming, I went to meet

you. And you appeared to me like a giant armed with furi-ous tempests, fighting the past by means of the present, overturning the old to the advantage of the new, and let-ting the strong scatter the weak.

In this way, I learned that the law of Man is your law. I learned that he who does not break up his branches dried out by his own tempest will die of indifference. And he who does not rebel to make his own dead leaves fall will perish from indolence.

Immense are your gifts, Earth, and deep are your groans; long too are the languishings of your heart for your chil-dren who have been led astray by their greed on the path of their truth.

We cry out to each other, and you smile.

We go astray, and you pay the penalty for us.

We soil things, and you sanctify.

And we blaspheme, and you bless.

We sleep without ever dreaming, and you dream in your eternal wakefulness. We speak to you while piercing your breast with swords and lances, and you heal our wound-like words with the scented oil of your waters.

We sow our bones and skulls in the palm of your hand, and you make willows and cypresses grow. We store our refuse and excrement within your caves and you fill our attics and taverns. We disfigure you with our blood and you wash our hands in the Eden river. We dissect your entrails in order to extract cannon and rockets from them, and from our bones your create the lily and the dew.

Earth, you are long-suffering and magnanimous.

And the Earth cries out to the soil:

"I am the womb and the sepulcher and I shall remain thus until the stars fade away and the sun turns into ashes."

The Weeping Stream

At daybreak, at the hour when men are resting peacefully beneath the mantle of sleep, I was sitting in a field and conversing with Nature.

In my contemplations I was transported far from any region inhabited by man, and there my imagination lifted the veil of matter which concealed my intimate being. My soul opened out, and there I was in the bosom of Nature and its secrets. My ears could then hear the secret language of its marvels.

Then I heard the stream lamenting, as a widow weeps over her dead child, and I asked; "Why are you weeping, stream of the limpid waters?"

And the stream replied: "I have to run through the city where men treat me with scorn and reject me, much preferring more intoxicating drinks. They will transform me into the refuse collector of their rubbish, they will pollute my purity and change my goodness into infection."

Earth and Man

Fire, storms, and earthquakes are to the Earth what envy, hatred, and evil are to the heart of Man.

I have seen Man, throughout his history, construct towers, palaces, cities, and temples everywhere on Earth. I have seen Earth turn in fury against these edifices and seize hold of them in order to absorb them back again into its bosom.

I have understood that Earth was like a sublime bride, having no need of the jewels carved by the hand of Man in order to complete her beauty, for she is content with the green grass of the fields, the golden sand of the beaches, and the precious stones of the mountains.

And among the ruins of Babylon, Nineveh, Palmyra, and Pompeii I have seen Man still standing, like a pillar of light. And I hear him again intoning the song of immortality:

"Let Earth take what belongs to it.

For I, Man, have no end."

Cities

O people of the noisy city, you who live in darkness, you whose sky is artificial, your towns are colossal cages for which men began to forge the bars many years ago, without realizing they were building them from the inside, and that soon they would be their own prisoners for eternity.

The people of the city pretend to be wise and knowing.

But their imagination remains unreliable, for they are none other than experts in imitation.

He who wishes to live in a busy town must be a sharp sword in a scabbard of honey.

The sword will serve him to repulse those who wish to kill time, and the honey will satisfy their hunger.

Nature holds out her welcoming arms to us and invites us to enjoy her beauty.

But we are afraid of her silence as we rush into the crowded towns, where we herd together like sheep fleeing the wicked wolf.

Work

My would took me to task and told me: "Do not rejoice at praise and do not despair at reproaches."

Before my soul gave me this advice I was doubtful about the value of my work.

Now I understand that trees flower in the spring and bear fruit in the summer without seeking praise.

And they let their leaves fall in the autumn and become bare in the winter without fearing blame.

Money

Money is like a stringed instrument. He who does not know how to use it skillfully will hear only discordant notes.

Money is like love: it kills slowly and painfully the man who keeps it and gladdens the man who shares it.

Yet love is the source of faith; as for money, it is the source of love without faith.

Eating and Drinking

Some of you, when you sit down to table, eat quickly, and when you walk, move forward slowly.

It would be preferable for you to eat with your feet and walk with your hands.

Beauty

Beauty is not in the face.
    Beauty is a light in the heart.

Have we then never heard it said, or seen it ourselves, that superficial beauty is sometimes responsible for many unknown but terrible calamities, and for so many profound and painful afflictions?
    Is that moon which inspires poets not the same moon that breaks up the calm of the waters with ebb and flow?

The most subtle beauties of our life are invisible and inaudible.

Believe in the divinity of Beauty which inspires your cult of Life and your aspiration to Happiness.

Art

Art is a step taken from the visible known to the secret unknown, from nature towards the infinite.

Music

Music is the quivering of a string, charged with waves from the upper air, it penetrates your hearing, its echo emerges from your eyes in a burning tear, and from your lips as they sigh for a beloved being far away, or it utters a moan caused by the sting of history and the fangs of destiny.

And it can happen that the notes of music are reflected on your lips in a smile of fulfillment.

Music is a houri in the paradise of the gods, who was in love with the sons of Adam. Then she came down to earth and told them of her love. The gods, in a fury, ordered a terrible wind to rush after her in pursuit.

In this way she was scattered through the air and disseminated to all the corners of the earth. She did not die, she still lives in the ears of humans.

Music is the echo of the first kiss bestowed by Adam on the lips of Eve. And ever since then this echo has caused pleasure to rebound onto fingers as they play and ears as they listen.

Through the eyes of hearing I was able to see the heart of love.

Music is the language of the spirit. Its melody is like a playful breeze which makes the strings vibrate with love.

When the fairy fingers of music touch the doorway of feelings they awake memories enclosed in the depths of the past.

O divine Music!

We lay our hearts and our souls closely within you.

You teach us to see with our ears, and to listen with our hearts.

The Nay

Give me the Nay* and sing,
The secret song of eternity.
The laments of the Nay will linger
Beyond the decline of existence.

Have you, like me,
Chosen the forest dwelling
Rather than the castle?
Have you followed the stream
And climbed the rocks?
Have you anointed your body
With fragrance distilled in light?
Have you been drunk with dawn
In the goblets full of pure air?

---

* A reed flute played by the dervishes during the sessions of *dhikr*,
and which, especially during the spiritual oratorio *Sâma*, sym-
bolizes the soul that is separated from its divine origin and aspires,
lamenting, to return there.

Have you, like me,
Sat down at dusk,
Among the glowing languor
Of vines laden with grapes?
Have you lain down on the grass at night
And covered yourself with the heavens,
Opening your heart to the future,
Forgetful of the past?

Give me the Nay and sing,
The song in tune with hearts.
The laments of the Nay will linger
Beyond the fading of sins.

Give me the Nay and sing,
Unmindful of troubles and cures.
For each man
Is nothing more than a watercolor sketch.

Poetry

Poetry is the sacred incarnation of a smile and a sigh which dries tears.

It is a spirit which settles in the soul whose heart is nourishment and whose wine is affection.

Poetry which does not appear in this form is a false Messiah.

Poet, examine your crown of thorns and you will see that within it is concealed a living crown of laurel.

O true poets, forgive us.

We belong to the new world where men pursue material possessions.

Poetry, today, is a consumer product and not a breath of immortality.

If the spirits of Homer, Virgil, Al-Maary, and Milton had known that poetry would become the lap-dog of the rich, they would have left the world, their tongues and their ears would have been cut off, their pens and their writings burned.

Counsel

Seek counsel from each other, for such is the way to end error and meaningless repentance. The wisdom of the multitude is your shield against tyranny. And each time you turn towards someone to receive his counsel, you reduce accordingly the number of your enemies.

Ask counsel from people wrinkled with age.

Their eyes have looked the years directly in the face, and their ears have listened to the voices of Life.

And even if their counsel were to displease you, do not fail to give them a little of your attention.

Wisdom

Learn the words of wisdom uttered by the sages and apply them within your life. Live them out, but do not declaim them, for whoever repeats what he has not understood is as useless as a donkey laden with books.

Step back, wisdom that does not weep,
philosophy that does not laugh,
and greatness that does not bow down before children.

Invitation from Wisdom

In the silent night came Wisdom.

She stopped near my bed and looked at me with the eyes of a loving mother. Then, drying my tears, Wisdom said to me:

"I have heard the sobbing of your spirit and I have come to console you.

"Open your heart to me, and I shall fill it with light.

"Ask me the way to truth, and I shall show it to you."

And I replied to her invitation with these questions:

"O Wisdom, who am I, and by what path did I reach this fearful place? Tell me, what are these hopes, these multiple writings, and these strange forms?

"What are these thoughts that traverse the dome of my consciousness like flights of pigeons? What is this poetry of passions, this prose of desires?

"What is this mingling of sorrowful influences and joyous responses which embrace my soul and clasp my heart? Whose are these eyes which plumb my depths and yet flee before my sorrows?

"What are these voices, sometimes regretful in memory of my past days and sometimes melodious in memory of my childhood? What is this youth which plays with my desires and laughs at my feelings, uncaring about the deeds of yesterday, glad of the pettiness of today, and disdainful of the slowness of tomorrow?

"What is this world that is leading me I know not where, humiliated like me by the worst ignominies? What is this earth with its gaping jaws, this greedy earth opening out to absorb our bodies and install its greediness within them?

"Who is this man, he who is satisfied with the zenith of fortune, without being wedded to its depths, who dares to beg for a kiss on the cheek of life, although his face has been struck by death?

"Who is this man, he who buys a moment of pleasure with a year of repentance and falls asleep when dreams summon him?

"Who is this man, he who is borne away on floods of ignorance towards the caverns of darkness?

"O Wisdom, tell me, what are all these things?"

And Wisdom answered me:

"Man likes to contemplate the world with the eyes of a god and to penetrate the secrets of the beyond by means of human thought; and this is no more than sheer stupidity.

"Go into the fields and watch the honeybee fly over the flowers and, in the distance, watch the eagle swoop down on its prey.

"Go into your neighbor's dwelling and admire the child who is fascinated by the fire in the hearth while his mother does the housework.

"Be like the honeybee and do not waste in vain your springtime days in watching the comings and goings of the eagle. Be like the child who rejoices in those flames and leaves his mother to her tasks.

"Everything that you see is yours for all time.

"Those countless books, those strange images, and those fine thoughts are only phantoms of spirits who have lived long before you.

"Those words that you weave are so many threads in the cloth that binds you to other people.

"Those happy or unhappy events are the seeds sown by the past in the field of your soul so that the future can harvest them.

"That youthfulness which juggles with your desires: is it not that youthfulness which will open the door of your heart so that light can enter it?

"This earth with its voracious craving: is it not this earth that will deliver your soul from the servitude of the body?

"This world that goes forward along with you: is it not your heart? And is not your heart the universe?

"That man whom you judge to be so mediocre and so ignorant, did he not spring from the bosom of God in order to teach you happiness within sorrow and to acquire knowledge through ignorance?

Thus spoke Wisdom.

Then, Wisdom placed a hand on my burning forehead and said to me:

"Go forward and do not stand still. For to go forward is to go towards perfection. Walk without fearing the thorns or the sharp stones which lie along the path of life, for they harm only impure blood."

Faith

Is faith not the sense of the heart just as sight is the sense of the eye?

God has created several doors which open onto truth.

He opens them to all those who knock on them with the hand of faith.

Good and Evil

Remember that a single just man causes the demon more trouble than a thousand blind believers.

Prayer

The sympathy which lightly touches the heart of your neighbor is more essential than the virtue that is hidden in the invisible recesses of a convent.

A word of compassion addressed to a criminal or a prostitute is more noble than the long and meaningless prayer that we repeat each day in the temples.

Religion

Religion is a ploughed field, sown and irrigated by the desire of someone who aspires to paradise or by someone who fears hell.

And, without the one need to draw up accounts of our debts on the day of the last judgment, you would not have worshipped God and you would not have repented in order to obtain a better fate.

As if religion were a commercial product in your daily transactions; neglecting it will ruin you, preserving it will bring you profit.

I love you, my brother, whoever you are.

I love you as you pray in your mosque, as you practice your devotions in church, or worship in your temple. For you and I are the children of one single religion: Faith.

And the varying pathways of religion represent the different fingers of the single loving hand of the Supreme Being. And this hand is stretched out towards us with ardor and offers us all the fulfillment of the Spirit.

A priest is often a traitor who uses Scriptures as a threat to spirit away your money, a hypocrite who carries a crozier and uses it like a sword to open your veins, a wolf in sheep's clothing, a glutton who has more respect for the table than for the altar, a creature hungry for gold who follows the dinar to the most distant countries.

He is a strange being, with the beak of an eagle, the claws of tiger, the teeth of a hyena, and the skin of a viper.

Take his Bible away from him, rend his vestments, pull out his beard, and do as you wish with him. Then place a dinar in his hand, and he will thank you with a smile.

God

The drop of dew curled up in the heart of the lily is no different from you when you deliver your soul into the heart of God.

Without doubt we are closer to God each time we try to divide him and find he is indivisible.

Most religions speak of God in the masculine; in my eyes he is as much a mother as a father.

He is a father and mother in one single Person, and Woman is his Mother-Goddess.

And we can be united to God the Father through the mind, but the Mother-Goddess can only be reached through the heart, through love.

Again I Dreamed of Jesus

It was in the Lebanon, where I always see him, in a village in the sacred valley of Qadicha. I was gathering watercress beside a little stream. And he arrived, his face always the same, with those wonderful dark, clear eyes, a sunburned face. He came from the East, and the light of the setting sun made his whole body glow.

I offered him watercress with both hands and said to him: "Master, would you like a little watercress?"

And he took it, still wet, raising it to his mouth. His smiling face seemed to widen as though a thousand wings were transporting him. And he ate with pleasure, as though the coolness delighted him. And he said: "Nothing is more beautiful than what is green and fresh."

Then he bent down to drink water from the stream. And when he stood up again the water was dripping from his beard and moustache, but he did not wipe it away.

And he left, looking at me with a gentle smile, as though happy at having shared this moment of pleasure.

Jesus of Nazareth

Jesus did not come from the heart of the Circle of Lights to destroy our dwellings and build convents and monasteries over their ruins, nor to persuade men to become priests or pastors.

But he came to breathe into the air of this earth a spirit as powerful as it was new, with the strength to undermine the foundations of all the monarchies erected over the bones of mankind.

He came here to demolish the majestic palaces constructed over the tombs of the weak and to destroy the statues erected over the corpses of the poor.

Jesus did not come to teach men how to build huge cathedrals and opulent temples close to humble cottages and cold, dark, homes.

But he came to make the heart of man into a temple, his soul into an altar, and his spirit into a priest.

O Jesus, to your honor and glory they built those churches and those cathedrals, adorned them with silk and melted down the golden calf over their cupolas.

They filled the sky with the smoke of candles and incense, while leaving your faithful worshippers without bread.

They intoned hymns of praise, while remaining deaf to the cries and tears of widows and orphans.

O Living Jesus, if only you could return to chase the merchants of Faith out of your sacred temple! For they made it into a dark cavern where the vipers of hypocrisy and trickery crawl in their thousands.

Lazarus and His Beloved

There is neither dream nor awakening down here. You, I, and this garden are only illusion, a shadow of reality. Awakening and reality are where I was with my beloved.

My beloved is my twin heart.

I had thought that she might have been down here, but I had not encountered her. Then death came like an angel with winged feet and led my ardent desire towards hers.

Then I lived with her within the very heart of God. I bound myself to her, and she to me. We were one single being, a sphere glistening in the sun, a melody in the stars.

My beloved and I were in space. We were the whole of space. We wandered like the former spirit of God, floating on the surface of the waters. And it was always the first day. We were love itself, dwelling in the heart of milky silence.

We were all that, all that and much more, until a voice, a voice from the depths, a voice from the world, summoned me. A voice like a clap of thunder, a voice like innumerable spears cutting through the upper air then rang out and echoed in space. And as for me, my flow became an ebb tide, a divided home, a torn garment, and an unlived youth. I became a tower about to collapse, and a boundary was marked out round those cracked and broken stones. I went down from the castle of the sky to a tomb which was inside another tomb. I went back into my body, into that other tomb that was laid out in a sealed cavern.

The inseparable was disunited; and the unending millennia lived out in the air with my beloved could not save me from the power of that voice, which summoned me to return to the earth: *Lazarus, rise and walk.*

Everything is so different on the other side of the valley. There are no weights, no measures. One is alone with one's beloved. O, my beloved! O, beloved fragrance breathed out into space! O, wings separated from me! Would our separation be difficult for you? Beloved, tell me, might there have been a twofold act of cruelty? Might you have been summoned back from death to life by another brother of Jesus from another world? Would another mother, other sisters and friends, have regarded that as a miracle?

O my Beloved, a dawn shone in your eyes and a mysterious silence was hidden in that dawn; that silence was the tranquility of a profound night and the promise without words of a long day. And I was overwhelmed with happiness and peace.

O my Beloved, that veil called life is between us now. Must I live that death again and die another time in order to be born anew? Must I still linger on this earth waiting for all green things to become yellow and bare? Why among all the shepherds am I the only one to be led back to the desert after being in the verdant pastures?

You, your neighbors as well as your fathers and your ancestors, would have liked to be present at a miracle in order to believe in the simple things of life. How cruel you are! What cruelty of heart! How dark is the nighttime in your eyes! So it is for this that you snatch the prophets from their fame for your own satisfaction and then you kill them.

You are in a house and under a roof. You are surrounded by four walls, with a door and a window. You are here, and you are deprived of all vision. Your reason is here, and my spirit is up there. Your entire being is on earth, while the whole of mine is in the air. You creep about your homes, while I fly above the mountaintops. You worship only yourselves. You sleep and you never dream. You are awake and you never walk over the hills. Yesterday, weary of your company and your lives, I searched for the other world which you call "death." But I did not desire death. And today I am here, standing before you, and I rebel against what you call "life."

Yes, it was my mother's sadness as well as yours which made me come back to earth. It was pity, self-pity which made me come back. How selfish is this self-pity and how deep!

The master summoned me back so that you could learn that there is no veil between life and death. His words uttered through love brought together the elements of myself which had been disseminated by death. In this way I have become a living witness of immortality.

He restored life to me, he gave you my life. He took my life away from my Beloved, he gave it to you. He wrought this miracle so that your eyes would be opened and your ears could hear. He sacrificed me as he sacrificed himself. Father, forgive them for they know not what they do. The master spoke these words as much for me as for himself, as well as for all the unknown people who know how to understand, but who are misunderstood. Did he not speak those words when your tears begged him to intercede in order to save my life? It is your burning desire and not his will which invited his spirit to the sealed door, delivering me into your arms.

I navigated through the wind on the open sea and braved the fury of the oceans in search of the blessed isles. What was that other wind which made me change course? And why did I return towards these shores? It was Jesus of Nazareth who controlled the wind with his own breath. It was he who breathed and made the wind fill my empty sails.

O, Jesus my friend, once, at table, you gave me a goblet of wine and said to me: "Drink this in memory of me." Then you dipped a piece of bread in the oil while saying to me: "Eat that, for it is my share of the bread." O, my friend, you placed your arm on my shoulder and you called me son. My mother and my sisters said within their hearts: "He loves our Lazarus." And I, I truly loved you. Tell me now, why did you make me come back to earth? Did you not know in your understanding heart that I was with my Beloved? Did you not meet her during your wanderings over the mountaintops of Lebanon? Would you not by chance have a Beloved in heaven? Would you separate from a "self" greater than your own self? And what would you have said after the separation? What should I say now?

Jesus of Nazareth, tell me now, why did you do this? Was it fair that I should be sacrificed in order to lay a small, modest, and grieving stone on the road which would lead others to the heights of your glory? Would any other death have served to glorify you? Why did you separate the lover from his Beloved? Why did you summon me back to a world which, as you knew in your heart, you would have to leave one day? Why did you summon me back from the living heart of eternity to a life worse than death?

Since you have been resuscitated from among the dead, I shall follow you until you give me death. From now on I shall seek your spirit and I shall be liberated. And although they will try to bind me with their chains, I shall remain free. No matter if thousands of mothers and thousands of sisters huddle against me, they will not hold me back. I shall go with the wind from the East wherever it goes. I shall search during the night, when all the mornings are still drowsy. I shall be the only man who has suffered life twice over, death twice over, the only man who will have known eternity twice.

Time

Tomorrow is conceived in the womb of yesterday.

Supreme Sea

How distant yesterday can be, as distant as it is close!

In company with my soul I was walking yesterday along the shores of that vast sea in search of a secluded bay where, far from onlookers, I could wash our body which the earth had covered with mud and dust.

However, we saw a man seated on an ashen rock, taking salt out of his pouch and casting it, one pinch at a time, onto the breaking waves.

Then my soul said to me: "That is the pessimist who sees only his shadow. I shall certainly not allow him to see our naked body. So let us leave this place."

We walked on until we reached an inlet of the sea. There, standing on a milky-looking rock we saw a man holding a box sparkling with jewels from which he was taking sugar and throwing it into the sea.

"That is the optimist who rejoices at every omen. He should not see our nudity either. Let us go, we cannot bathe here," my soul avowed to me.

We continued on our way. And there was a man picking up dead fish from the sand and tenderly putting them back in the water.

And my soul described him: "He is the philanthropist who tries to restore life to the tombs. Let us move away from him."

And farther on still we saw a man tracing the outline of his shadow on the sand and the waves washing it away. At once he traced it again, and again the sea washed it away.

"That is the mystic who cherishes illusions and builds them up into statues to be worshipped," my soul told me, "he does not deserve to see us naked either."

And farther away still we caught sight of another man scooping up foam with his hand and pouring it into an alabaster goblet.

"That is the idealist. He weaves his clothes out of spider's webs. He is certainly not worthy of seeing our nudity," said my soul.

Again we walked on. And suddenly we heard a voice crying out: "It is the sea, the profound sea. O you, who are boundless and full of power." On arriving at the place from where this voice emerged we saw a man with his back to the sea, holding a shell to his ear. He was listening to the memory of the waves.

And my soul said: "Let us not stay here. He is the realist. He turns his back on the unfathomable infinite and enthuses over insignificant trifles."

So we went on. And farther along on the beach there was a man with his head buried in the sand.

Then I said to my soul: "At last we know where to bathe. This man cannot see us."

"No, a thousand times no," objected my soul. "This ostrich is the worst man we have met all along the beach. He is the pious puritan who continually averts his eyes from the tragedy of life, and life renders him blind to all forms of happiness."

However, a great sadness came over my soul's face. And in a voice breaking with bitterness it said: "Let us go, for there is no secluded place along this shore where we can bathe. I shall not allow the zephyr to unveil my virgin breast, nor shall the wind lift my golden hair, and the light shall not reveal my sacred nudity."

We left this shore and we set out in search of the other sea, the supreme sea.

Perfection

Man will be on the path to perfection when his being becomes a universe without bounds and a sea without shores.

When he knows how to create eternal thunder and lightning, as soon as he becomes those gusts of wind or gentle breezes, or those clouds laden with lightning, heavy with thunder, and pregnant with rain, when he becomes those streams that are sometimes lively, sometimes sad, those trees in bud or shedding their leaves, those mountains which stand high or lie down in valleys, those fields under seed or lying fallow:

When man is aware of all this, he is already halfway along the path to perfection; and if he aspires to reach its summit, he will brush against the fulfillment of his existence.

He will have to embody the child crying in its mother's arms, the father concerned about his family, the young man wavering between desires and sighs, the old man struggling against the past and with the future, the devout man in his hermitage, the criminal in his jail, the scholar among his endless writings, the ignorant man stumbling against the shadows of the night and in the darkness of his days, the priestess surrounded with her blossoming faith and her thorny solitude, the prostitute caught between the fangs of weakness and the claws of need, the deprived man between fatality and honesty, the rich man between passion and reason, the poet between the mistiness of his nights and the clear light of his dawns.

If man can live out all these things, he will grasp perfection and will then become one of the shadows of God.

Death

The beginning of life is not in matter, and its end is not in the tomb. For the years that pass are only a moment in eternal life, while the world and matter and everything that composes it is only a dream in the sight of that awakening which you mistakenly call the terror of death.

Existence

Everything that exists endures forever, and the very existence of existence is the proof of eternity.

But without this understanding, which is the knowledge of the perfect being, man would never have known if there is an existence or a nonexistence.

If eternal existence is transformed, it should become more beautiful.

If it disappears, it must return with an aspect that is more sublime.

And if it sleeps, it must dream of a better awakening.

For each time that it is born anew it is greater.

Eternity

Humanity is a river of light which runs from the valleys of Creation down to the ocean of Eternity.

Between the peoples of eternity and the peoples of the earth there is constant communication. And we must obey the will of this invisible power.

Often an individual performs an act believing it takes place with his consent and on his orders, while in fact he has been precisely guided and inspired in order to accomplish it.

And a great number of men have achieved fame by abandoning themselves to the will of the spirit in proud submission, without objecting and without resisting its demands, as the violin abandons itself totally to the will of a good musician.

Between the world of the spirit and the world of matter there is a pathway that we tread as though we were half-asleep. It supports our steps but we are not conscious of its strength. And when we awake we shall discover that we are carrying in our own hands the seeds we must carefully sow in the good soil of our daily life so that they will produce our good actions and our finest words.

If there were not this pathway between our lives and the lives of those who have left us, there would never have been among us any prophet, poet, or genius.

❧

They only return to Eternity who have sought it on earth.

Words of the Master

My writings are no more than a handful of sand, a handful of foam, although in its grains of sand I have sown the seeds of my heart and poured the quintessence of my soul over its foam.

My writings are and will remain forever closer to the shore than to the sea, closer to the desire which burns to fulfill itself rather than to the desire which is burned out as soon as it is accomplished.

In the heart of every man and every woman there is a little sand along with a little foam.

But some among us yield up what remains concealed in the plumage of their hearts, while others are ashamed to do so.

As for me, I feel no shame at all.

I am often called the gravedigger. And some people believe that I am violent and destructive.

But I cannot build without destroying. We humans are like walnuts: we have to be broken open before we can be discovered. Emery paper could fulfill this task, but it would need a great deal of time, for light caresses cannot awaken people.

❧

Do no call me wise, unless you call all men wise.

I am merely an unripe fruit still hanging on the branch, only yesterday I was still a flower.

The Death of the Prophet

I fly away into the air, towards the court of the spirits, and I shall return to this world. For Ishtar restores life to loving spirits who have been torn away by the hands of eternity before they can enjoy all the delights of love and all the happiness of youth.

The generations which pass and pulverize the works of man in no way cause his dreams to perish or his aspirations to weaken.

Dreams and aspirations will last as long as the universality of the eternal soul exists. Sometimes they disappear, sometimes they fall half-asleep, like the sun at dusk or the moon at dawn.

We shall see each other again and we shall drink the morning dew from the cups of the narcissus flowers.

My brothers on earth, I bequeath to you my last sigh.

I abandon myself to eternal sleep, and my blessed soul floats over you now in the heaven of the spirit, far from all sorrow and sadness. My soul has freed itself from the servitude of the body and from the burdens of earthly life.

I am leaving the material world and rejoining a new world which knows neither torments nor afflictions. My new dwelling, into which your gaze cannot penetrate and your ears are not admitted, exists in the kingdom of the spirit where its presence is sorely needed.

I am educating myself from now on in a different universe, whose history and beauty have always captivated me and whose language I have always tried to learn.

My life on earth found repose only in work. And I loved work and I had called it *Love made Visible*.

My soul on earth was a source of knowledge emerging from the bosom of Eternity, a river of pure wisdom, attempting to water and refresh the spirit of man.

In future this river will bathe the banks of eternal Life. Let no importunate man come to lament my fate or shed tears over my departure.

For, remember, only those who have never penetrated into the Temple of Life, nor fertilized the soil with the slightest drop of sweat from their brows, deserve your tears and lamentations when they leave this earth.

It is fitting that genius should not receive from you, but give to you. This is the only way you have of honoring him.

Do not weep over my death, but rejoice and drink your fill at the spring of my wisdom.

❧

I shall be a child leaning against the bosom of Karima.

Sources

The writings in this book have been selected from French translations of the following works of Kahlil Gibran.

Published in Arabic by Sadir, Beirut:
Music, 1905.
The Nymphs of the Valley, 1906.
The Rebel Minds, 1908 (French translation ed. Dangles).
Broken Wings, 1912 (French translation ed. Mortagne).
Tears and Smiles, 1914.
The Processions, 1919.
The Storms, 1920.
Marvels and Curiosities, 1923.

Letters of Kahlil Gibran:
Al-Shu'la al-Zarqa, Al-Kusbari, and Bashru'i, Damascus.
Rasâ'il Gibrân, Beirut.

Works translated into French:
La Voix e l'éternelle sagesse (ed. Dangles).
Les Secrets du Coeur (ed. Mortagne).

Autoportrait (ed. Mortagne).
Les Trésors de la sagesse (ed. Mortagne).
La Voix du maître (ed. Mortagne).
Les Miroirs de l'âme (ed. Mortagne).
Pensées et Méditations (ed. Mortagne).
L'Envol de l'esprit (ed. Mortagne).